P9-DCD-647

WITHDRAWN

GAME DAY: FOOTBALL

QUARTERBACKS

WEST PALM BEACH PUBLIC LIBRARY
411 CLEMATIS STREET
WEST PALM BEACH, FL 33401
(561) 868-7700

By K.C. Kelley

Reading consultant: Cecilia Minden-Cupp, Ph.D.,
Literacy Specialist

Gareth Stevens
Publishing

Please visit our web site at www.garethstevens.com.
For a free describing Gareth Stevens Publishing's list of high-quality books, call 1-800-542-2595 (USA) or 1-800-387-3178 (Canada). Gareth Stevens Publishing's fax: 1-877-542-2596

Library of Congress Cataloging-in-Publication Data
Kelley, K. C.
   Quarterbacks / by K.C. Kelley.
      p. cm. — (Game day. Football)
         Includes bibliographical references and index.
      ISBN-10: 1-4339-1961-3 — ISBN-13: 978-1-4339-1961-9 (lib. bdg.)
      1. Quarterbacks (Football)—United States—Biography—Juvenile literature.
      2. Quarterbacking (Football)—United States—Juvenile literature. I. Title.
   GV939.A1K45   2010
   796.3320922—dc22 [B]   2008055596

This edition first published in 2010 by
Gareth Stevens Publishing
A Weekly Reader® Company
1 Reader's Digest Road
Pleasantville, NY 10570-7000 USA

Copyright © 2010 by Gareth Stevens, Inc.

Executive Managing Editor: Lisa M. Herrington
Senior Editor: Brian Fitzgerald
Senior Designer: Keith Plechaty

Produced by Q2AMedia
Art Direction: Rahul Dhiman
Senior Designer: Dibakar Acharjee
Image Researcher: Kamal Kumar

Photo credits
Key: t = top, b = bottom, c = center, l = left, r = right
Cover and title page: Travis Lindquist/Getty Images
Elaine Thompson/Associated Press: 4; Drew Hallowell/Getty Images: 5; Bettmann/Corbis: 6–7; Focus On Sport/Getty Images: 8; Al Messerschmidt/The Sports Gallery: 9, 9br; Bettmann/Corbis: 10, 11; Al Messerschmidt/The Sports Gallery: 12, 13, 14, 15, 16, 16bl, 17; Grant Halverson/Getty Images: 18; David Stluka/Getty Images: 19; Twig/NYCSportsPics: 19br, 20, 21; David Drapkin/Getty Images: 22; Twig/NYCSportsPics: 23; Gregory Shamus/Getty Images: 24; Stephen Dunn/Getty Images: 25; Jim McIsaac/Getty Images: 26; Drew Hallowell/Getty Images: 27; Al Messerschmidt/The Sports Gallery: 28; David Drapkin/Getty Images: 29; Michael Fabus/Getty Images: 30; Andy Lyons/Getty Images: 31; Al Messerschmidt/The Sports Gallery: 32; Chris McGrath/Getty Images: 33; Al Messerschmidt/The Sports Gallery: 34; Scott Boehm/Getty Images: 35; Twig/NYCSportsPics: 36–37; Rex Brown/Getty Images: 38; Focus on Football: 39; Mike Eliason: 40, 41, 42; Al Messerschmidt/The Sports Gallery: 44; Twig/NYCSportsPics: 45.
Q2AMedia Art Bank: 7br, 43

All rights reserved. No part of this book may be reproduced, stored in a retrieval system, or transmitted in any form or by any means, electronic, mechanical, photocopying, recording, or otherwise, without the prior written permission of the copyright holder. For permission, contact **permissions@gspub.com**.

Printed in the United States of America

CPSIA Compliance Information: Batch#CR909011GS: For further information contact Gareth Stevens, New York, New York at 1-800-542-2595

Cover: Eli Manning of the New York Giants is one of the top quarterbacks in pro football.

Contents

Words in the glossary appear in **bold** type the first time they are used in the text.

Touchdown!

The quarterback, or QB, is the most important player on a football field. Here's a story of a real-life quarterback using his skills to win the big game. In this book, you will read about all these skills and more!

TIME FOR A BIG PLAY!

In February 2008, New York Giants quarterback Eli Manning had less than two minutes to win the Super Bowl. His team trailed the New England Patriots 14–10. He knew he had to make a big play. He took the snap from the center. He dropped back to pass. Suddenly, Manning was swarmed by Patriots. They pulled at his shirt and grabbed his legs. He **scrambled** to escape them. He set his feet and threw a long pass. Giants receiver David Tyree was there to make a super catch!

▼ Eli Manning (10) escapes from the defense before his famous pass to David Tyree.

▲ Eli Manning holds up the championship trophy. Giants head coach Tom Coughlin (clapping) joins the celebration.

TIME TO WIN!

Manning and the Giants were not in the end zone yet. Tyree's catch moved them to the 24-yard line. A few plays later, it was time for another Manning miracle. He led his team to the **line of scrimmage**. He got the ball and threw it to the back of the end zone. Manning knew his teammate Plaxico Burress would be there. Burress made a great catch! The Giants were National Football League (NFL) champions!

The quarterback is in the thick of the action on every play. Read on to learn more about this key position.

GLOSSARY

scrambled: ran away from pass rushers

line of scrimmage: the imaginary line that divides the offense and the defense before each play

CHAPTER

1

Birth of the Quarterback

Quarterbacks have not always been a part of football. In fact, for a long time, throwing a pass was against the rules!

A RUNNING GAME

Football began in the 1880s. The only way to move the ball forward was to carry it. Scores were very low. Running the ball so often was hard on runners, blockers, and tacklers. It was also pretty boring for the fans! Passing was allowed only if the ball was thrown backward as a **lateral**.

The forward pass was legalized in 1906. By the early 1910s, every team used passing plays. They needed a player to throw those passes. Quarterback soon became the game's most important position.

▶ Crunch! Here's action from the early, hard-hitting days of the NFL. Players wore canvas pants and very little padding.

Players wore leather helmets until the 1940s.

Lining Up

Football teams have dozens of **formations**. When you watch a game, look for different formations. For example, does the team have one receiver on either end of the line? Or does it put two on one side and one on the other? The team might also have a "man in motion." That is a player who runs along the line until the ball is snapped. Some formations are better for running plays. Others are better for passing plays.

FANCY FOOTBALL

Coaches began to arrange their teams on the field in different ways. Some formations made it easier to pass. Teams used these new formations to help them score. The "T" formation came along in the 1940s. It has changed slightly to become today's Pro Set offense (see diagram).

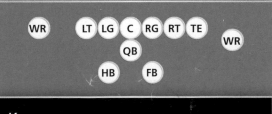

Key

WR: Wide Receiver	RT: Right Tackle
LT: Left Tackle	TE: Tight End
LG: Left Guard	QB: Quarterback
C: Center	HB: Halfback
RG: Right Guard	FB: Fullback

GLOSSARY

lateral: a pass that travels backward. A team is allowed one forward pass per play, but there is no limit on laterals.

formations: the ways that football teams line up their players on the field

EVERYBODY GO LONG!

In 1960, the American Football League (AFL) was formed. The new league wanted to take on the older and popular NFL. AFL teams played very entertaining football. Long passes were a big part of most offenses. The AFL featured many exciting quarterbacks. **Bombs**, or long passes, soon became popular among NFL teams, too.

◄ Len Dawson was one of the AFL's top quarterbacks. He led the league in touchdown passes four times. He guided the Kansas City Chiefs to Super Bowls I and IV.

The quarterback holds out his non-throwing hand for balance.

GLOSSARY

bombs: long, high passes that often lead to touchdowns

◄ Coach Bill Walsh (left) worked with star quarterback Joe Montana on the San Francisco 49ers.

WEST COAST RULES!

The passing game changed again in the early 1980s. The "West Coast" offense was developed by Bill Walsh and other coaches. In that offense, teams use quick, short passes to move the ball. Many teams use the West Coast offense today.

The Mad Bomber

AFL star Daryle Lamonica was one of the best long passers ever. He played quarterback for the Oakland Raiders. Lamonica was known as "the Mad Bomber."

QB Legends

As the passing game became more important, many quarterbacks became stars. Let's meet some great quarterbacks of the past.

SUPER SAMMY

"Slingin'" Sammy Baugh played for the Washington Redskins from 1937 to 1952. He led the Redskins to two NFL championships. Baugh was an awesome athlete. He played quarterback, **defensive back**, and punter. In fact, in 1943, he led the NFL in passing, **interceptions**, and punting!

GLOSSARY

defensive back: a defensive player who is usually assigned to cover a receiver

interceptions: passes that are caught by the defense

A REAL WINNER!

A quarterback's job is to help his team win. No QB did that better than Otto Graham of the Cleveland Browns. In 10 years (1946–1955), he led the Browns to a championship game 10 times. They won seven of them. Graham was a great passer and a tough player. He once got hit in the face on one play and threw a touchdown pass on the next.

Where's the Facemask?

Otto Graham (above) has a facemask. Sammy Baugh (left) doesn't. Why? Leather helmets came into use in the 1930s. They didn't have facemasks, however. Metal would not attach to the leather. When plastic helmets were created in the 1940s, metal bars were added. The bars helped protect players' faces. The first facemasks, like Graham's, were just one bar. Today, most facemasks have several bars.

JOHNNY U.

Johnny Unitas was famous for being able to rally his team when they were behind. In the 1958 NFL Championship Game, he led the Baltimore Colts to a legendary victory in **overtime**. He was not fast or super-strong, but he was a terrific passer and a respected leader. Unitas threw at least one touchdown pass in 47 games in a row. That's still a record. Unitas later helped the Colts win Super Bowl V.

Johnny Unitas wore small shoulder pads. He said big pads got in the way of his passing arm.

Johnny U. was known for wearing high-top shoes.

Scrambling Fran

Fran Tarkenton wasn't very tall, but he sure was quick. No one scrambled better than Tarkenton. He was also a great passer. His running and passing helped the Minnesota Vikings reach three Super Bowls in the 1970s. When Tarkenton retired, no one had more touchdown passes than him.

BROADWAY JOE

Quarterbacks can inspire teams to greatness. No one expected Joe Namath to lead his New York Jets to a win in Super Bowl III in 1969. The Colts were just too good, the experts said. "Broadway" Joe guaranteed a win! Then he backed up that promise by leading the Jets to a 16–7 victory.

▼ Joe Namath was the first pro QB to throw for 4,000 yards in a season. He had 4,007 in 1967.

GLOSSARY

overtime: an extra period that is played when a game is tied after 60 minutes. The first team to score in overtime wins the game.

SUPER JOE

Who was the greatest QB ever? Joe Montana is always near the top of the list. Montana led the San Francisco 49ers to four Super Bowl titles in the 1980s. He was the Most Valuable Player (MVP) of three of those games. His calm leadership and pinpoint passing turned his team into winners. Montana was not the biggest, strongest, or fastest player. He was just the best.

◄ Joe Montana was always calm under pressure. He earned the nickname "Joe Cool."

▶ Dan Marino was the Miami Dolphins
quarterback from 1983 to 1999.

MARINO MAGIC

A **quick release** means a passer gets rid of the ball in an instant. Dan Marino had the quickest release ever. He used his powerful throwing arm to set all-time records for touchdown passes and passing yards. Brett Favre later broke those marks. Still, Marino remains one of football's all-time greats.

GLOSSARY

quick release: for a QB, the ability to throw a pass before the defense reaches him

CAPTAIN COMEBACK

Quarterbacks need to come through when the game is on the line. No one did that better than John Elway of the Denver Broncos. He led the Broncos to 47 comeback wins in the fourth quarter. That's more than any other quarterback. Elway also led Denver to victories in back-to-back Super Bowls in the late 1990s.

▲ John Elway lost the first three Super Bowls he played in. He kept working hard and ended up a winner.

No. 8 = No. 1

Another great quarterback of the 1990s was Troy Aikman. He guided the Dallas Cowboys to three Super Bowl titles in four years. They were the first team to do that.

FABULOUS FAVRE

No player has thrown for more touchdowns or yards than Brett Favre. He is the only player to win three straight NFL MVP awards (1996–1998). He is not only super-talented, he is also tough. How tough? Through 2008, Favre started 269 games in a row for the Green Bay Packers and the New York Jets. He had to ignore big and small injuries to do it. Fans love his toughness, his talent, and his heart.

Why the towel? QBs use it to keep their hands dry. A dry hand means a better grip on the football.

► Brett Favre sets up to pass. In January 1997, he led Green Bay to a win in Super Bowl XXXI.

How to Play QB

Calling plays. Making passes. Handing off the ball. Leading his team. A QB has many jobs!

CALLING PLAYS

47 X-Slant, Y-Cross. That sounds like a code, right? Well, it is. Every team has hundreds of plays. Each play is known by a code. The QB tells his team the play in the **huddle**. He says the code clearly and quickly. Then he "breaks" the huddle by clapping his hands.

▼ Jake Delhomme of the Carolina Panthers calls a play in the huddle. He has a list of plays on his wristband.

HUT-HUT-HIKE!

In the huddle, the quarterback tells the team the **snap count**. That lets them know when the play will begin. The QB stands behind the center. He calls out signals. Some signals are meant to confuse the defense. Others are for his team. When the quarterback says a certain signal, the center snaps the ball. The play begins!

▲ Tony Romo of the Dallas Cowboys calls out signals.

TONY DUNGY

Coach to QB—Over!

NFL coaches can talk to their quarterbacks on the radio. The QB has an earpiece in his helmet. The coaches wear headsets (above). The coach calls in the play to the QB. The QB then tells the team.

GLOSSARY

huddle: the gathering of a team's players before each play

snap count: the words or numbers a QB calls out to start each play

Change of Plans

Coaches decide which play to run. But sometimes the QB changes the play at the line of scrimmage.

Passers use hand signals to make changes at the line.

▲ Peyton Manning of the Indianapolis Colts likes to change plays at the line of scrimmage.

SWITCHING UP

Sometimes the quarterback sees a defensive formation he doesn't like. When that happens, he can call an **audible**. He yells out a signal for a new play. When the ball is snapped, the team runs the new play. Quarterbacks must study their playbooks carefully to learn all the plays.

QB TALK

To make an audible, a QB will call out in code. He might say a color, such as "Blue! Blue!" He might call out a number and a direction, such as "33 Right!" He may also use hand signals to tell teammates about the new play.

Teams change hand signals each game to confuse the defense.

WHY CHANGE?

What makes a quarterback call an audible? Usually, it is because the defense made a move he didn't expect. A linebacker might be too close to the line. A defensive back might be too close to a receiver. The quarterback hopes the change will surprise the defense. Changing the play can be risky. If he makes the wrong call, his team might lose yardage—or the ball!

GLOSSARY

audible: a new play that the quarterback calls at the line of scrimmage

21

Passing

Quarterbacks need many skills. The most important is passing. QBs practice this skill more than any other.

HOLDING THE BALL

QBs hold the football toward one pointed end of the ball. Their fingertips are over the laces. Some players put their index finger on the point of the ball, too. They hold the ball firmly but don't squeeze too tightly.

SETTING UP

Here is how a quarterback throws a perfect pass. First, he points the non-throwing shoulder toward the target. For a right-handed thrower, that is the left shoulder. He points his left foot toward the target, too. (A left-hander reverses the directions!) The passer's chest points toward the sideline.

ELI MANNING

QBs put two or three fingers across the laces. They use the index finger to guide the throw.

DROPPING BACK

Whether a QB gets the ball on a direct snap or in the **shotgun formation**, he drops back. He jogs backward to get a better view of the field. Most QBs cross their feet as they move, rather than shuffle them. Most plays call for the QB to drop back three to five steps.

The passing arm should form the letter "L." The elbow should be even with the shoulder.

The passer pushes off with his back foot. That gives him power for good throws.

STEP AND THROW

Next comes the fun part. The QB pulls the ball back about level with his ear. Then he pulls his throwing arm forward. The elbow comes first, followed by the forearm, and then the hand. As the ball leaves his hand, he pulls down and forward. That gives the ball spin. The spin makes the ball go straighter.

TOM BRADY

GLOSSARY

shotgun formation: a way that the offense lines up with the quarterback standing several feet behind the center

AIMING THE BALL

Good aim from passes comes from practice, of course. But it also takes perfect passing form. The steps on the previous pages are the best way to make sure passes get where they're supposed to go. Quarterbacks often study game film to help them improve their form.

▼ Tony Romo of the Cowboys throws a pass. He's aiming at the receiver on the far left of the photo. The receiver should be able to catch the ball without slowing down.

► Philip Rivers of the San Diego Chargers makes a throw on the run.

THROWING ON THE RUN

All quarterbacks want to throw from the **pocket**. They depend on their linemen to protect them from the defenders trying for a sack. However, sometimes a QB has to scramble before getting off a pass. Throwing on the run is harder and takes even more practice.

The QB-Receiver Team

Quarterbacks work very closely with their receivers. The key to their success is timing. A receiver can't just run to a spot and wait for the ball to arrive. The defense would be waiting there, too! He runs a planned **route** called by the quarterback in the huddle. The quarterback times his throw to arrive at a spot at the same time as the receiver. Sometimes, the ball is in the air even before the pass catcher turns around or makes his cut.

GLOSSARY

pocket: the area that blockers form around the quarterback when he drops back to pass

route: the path a receiver takes as he goes out for a pass

Handoffs

Quarterbacks don't pass on every play, of course. They also move the ball upfield by handing off to teammates.

STUFF IN THE GUT

Quarterbacks use handoffs to get the ball to running backs. After taking the snap, the QB spins toward a running back. He holds the ball in one hand. As the back runs forward, the QB stuffs the ball into the runner's midsection. The runner grabs the ball with both hands. He holds it tightly to his stomach as he runs into the line.

▼ Donovan McNabb of the Philadelphia Eagles shows perfect form as he hands off to running back Brian Westbrook.

Jason Campbell uses two hands to softly toss the ball to running back Clinton Portis. QBs pitch the ball in front of the runner so he can keep moving.

HERE'S THE PITCH!

The quarterback can get the ball to a running back on a pitch. That doesn't mean he's playing baseball! A pitch in football is a short, underhanded toss. It can go to the side or backward. The runner catches the ball as he moves. Then he keeps running up the field.

End-Around

The **end-around** is a tricky running play. On an end-around, a wide receiver sprints behind the QB instead of running downfield. The quarterback hands off the ball to him. The receiver-turned-runner streaks away!

GLOSSARY

end-around: a running play in which a wide receiver takes a handoff from the quarterback

Time to Run!

Sometimes a quarterback helps his team not by throwing the ball, but by running with it!

SCRAMBLING

When a quarterback has to run around to avoid tacklers it's called "scrambling." Some quarterbacks are very nimble and fast and become good scramblers. Most QBs, however, do not run well and try to scramble as little as possible.

To keep from fumbling, runners tuck the football tightly against their body.

▶ Jason Campbell of the Redskins tucks the ball into his body as he takes off downfield.

RUNNING QBS

Most runs by QBs are not planned. Some QBs are fast and tough enough to run the ball, though. Coaches call special plays to use these skills. One quarterback-only running play is the **bootleg**. The QB fakes a handoff one way. Then he turns and runs the other way. When he runs alone without blockers, it's called a "naked" bootleg!

The Colts have run a sneak. That's QB Peyton Manning under that pile of players—and over the goal line for a touchdown!

Sneaky!

Another QB running play is the **sneak**. A team calls a sneak when it needs less than a yard or is very close to the goal line. The QB takes the snap. He plunges headfirst into the line. He tries to break through the pile of players to move the ball forward.

GLOSSARY

bootleg: a run by the QB around the end of the line

sneak: a short run or plunge by the quarterback into the center of the line

Quarterbacks in Charge

Quarterbacks have to be more than great athletes. They have to be leaders.

LEADERSHIP

Being a great passer doesn't make a player a great quarterback. He needs to lead his team. He has to play hard and act confidently. That might mean telling a teammate to work harder. It might mean talking a coach into calling a certain play.

▼ Ben Roethlisberger of the Pittsburgh Steelers meets with his receivers on the sideline. Quarterbacks need to communicate well with their teammates.

AN INSPIRATION

The quarterback sets an example for the whole team. If he is upset, his teammates may act that way, too. He can't get mad at other players for making mistakes. He needs to shrug off minor injuries. He also encourages his teammates. No matter what happens, he has to remain calm and cool. If he does, then his teammates will, too.

► John Elway knew he was going to get hit at the end of this run. He also knew that his team needed him to make a big play.

A Good Example

The Broncos trailed the Packers in the third quarter of Super Bowl XXXII. John Elway knew he had to make a big play. He scrambled. He dove headfirst toward the **first-down marker**. Elway knew he would be smacked by two Green Bay defenders. He dove anyway. Elway was spun around in the air, and he landed hard. But he got the first down! That play charged up his team. The Broncos went on to win the game.

GLOSSARY

first-down marker: the pole on the sideline that shows where a team must reach to earn a first down

GOOD TIMING

A team needs its quarterback most during close games. That's when a great quarterback shines. When his team is ahead, a QB must protect the ball so his team can hang on for a win. When his team is behind, a QB must do whatever it takes to pull out a victory. He must complete an impossible pass or scramble for a key first down. He cannot fumble or throw an interception. Great players know when it's time to buckle down and succeed.

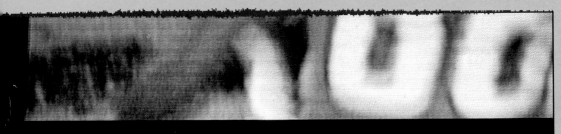

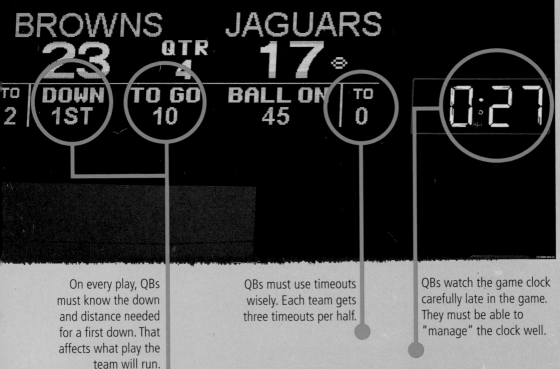

BROWNS 23   JAGUARS 17

QTR 4

TO	DOWN	TO GO	BALL ON	TO	0:27
2	1ST	10	45	0	

On every play, QBs must know the down and distance needed for a first down. That affects what play the team will run.

QBs must use timeouts wisely. Each team gets three timeouts per half.

QBs watch the game clock carefully late in the game. They must be able to "manage" the clock well.

THE TWO-MINUTE DRILL

All of a quarterback's skills come together during the **two-minute drill**. That is when a QB leads his team down the field late in the first half or in the fourth quarter. Eli Manning led a famous two-minute drill in Super Bowl XLII (pages 4–5). The QB must choose the right plays. He has to make the right throws. He has to bounce back quickly from big hits. And he has to inspire his team to win. Great quarterbacks do all these things and more.

◀ Cowboys QB Tony Romo (top) celebrates with tight end Jason Witten after they connected on a game-winning touchdown.

GLOSSARY

two-minute drill: a series of plays run late in the half or game that help a team move the ball quickly

QB Stars of Today

Now that you know what a quarterback does, let's meet some of today's superstars.

TOM TERRIFIC!

Tom Brady was the 199th player taken in the 2000 **NFL Draft**. All the teams that didn't choose him are kicking themselves now! Brady took over as the Patriots starter in 2001 and soon became a star. He led them to three Super Bowl championships in four seasons.

◄ Brady shows off his perfect passing form. He grips the ball properly as he looks downfield.

GLOSSARY

NFL Draft: a yearly meeting in which NFL teams select from the top college players

RECORD-SETTING SEASON

In 2007, Brady had the best season ever for a QB. He threw 50 touchdown passes, a new record! He led the Patriots to 18 straight wins. The first 16 were in the regular season. The Pats were the first team since 1972 to finish the regular season undefeated! Brady and the Patriots lost to Eli Manning and the Giants in Super Bowl XXLII.

Brady wears a wristband that lists his team's plays. Many QBs use wristbands to help them call plays in the huddle.

Super Sub

Backup quarterbacks must be ready at all times to step in and get the job done. Tom Brady hurt his knee and had to miss most of the 2008 season. The Patriots called on backup Matt Cassel. He took over and did a fine job. He threw for 21 touchdowns and passed for more than 3,600 yards. Cassel joined the Kansas City Chiefs for the 2009 season.

PEYTON MANNING

Being a great quarterback runs in the Manning family. Archie Manning played in the NFL for 13 seasons. His son Peyton has become one of the NFL's all-time greats. In 2004, Peyton threw for an amazing 49 touchdowns. He led the Colts to the playoffs five times before they finally won the Super Bowl in the 2006 season. Through 2008, Peyton had nine seasons with at least 4,000 passing yards. He was named NFL MVP following the 2003, 2004, and 2008 seasons.

ELI MANNING

Peyton Manning's younger brother is a star QB, too. Eli Manning joined the Giants in 2004. He struggled for a few seasons, but he didn't give up. His hard work paid off during the 2007 season. Eli put together a series of amazing playoff performances. He finished it off with the plays described on pages 4–5. He joined his brother as a Super Bowl champion.

DREW BREES

Another top NFL QB is Drew Brees. After five seasons with the San Diego Chargers, he joined the New Orleans Saints in 2006. Brees has a strong passing arm. In 2008, he became just the second QB to throw for 5,000 yards in a season. Brees also earned his third selection to the **Pro Bowl**, the NFL all-star game.

The "C" on Brees's jersey stands for "captain." NFL teams often choose their QB as one of the team captains.

BIG BEN

Ben Roethlisberger got off to a great start in his NFL career. As a **rookie** in 2004 he helped the Steelers win 15 games. The next season, he led them to a win in Super Bowl XL! During the 2008 season, he made the Steelers champions once again. With Pittsburgh trailing late in Super Bowl XLIII, he led the team more than 70 yards in two minutes. With less than a minute to play, he hit Santonio Holmes with the game-winning score! For Big Ben, two Super Bowl wins in four years is just the start!

GLOSSARY

Pro Bowl: the NFL's annual all-star game

rookie: a player in his first season of pro football

CHAPTER 5

Future Star: You!

Would you like to be a quarterback? Here are some ways to practice QB skills.

JUST PASS IT!

Quarterbacks need to practice passing more than any other skill. You can throw to a friend or at a target. When you pass, focus on using good form. Step toward your target with the foot opposite your passing arm. As you pull your arm forward, keep your elbow about level with your shoulder. As you are about to release the ball, your chest should point toward your target. Use your non-throwing arm for balance.

AIR IT OUT!

Place cones or hoops at different spots around the field, including some as far as you think can throw. Throw passes at the different objects to work on your distance. Try to have the ball land as close to the targets as possible. Then try this drill while throwing on the run.

Keep your fingers on the laces as you throw. This helps the ball go straighter.

MOVING TARGETS

Passing to a receiver who is running can be tricky. The quarterback has to learn to "lead" the receiver. The quarterback throws the ball in front of the receiver. That way the receiver can catch it without stopping. Practice this skill with a friend. Have him or her run across the field. Try to throw the ball so your friend can catch it while still running.

◄ A good quarterback throws the ball in front of the receivers. That lets them catch with their hands away from their body.

PASSING TREE

A good QB needs to memorize a lot of plays. This diagram, called a **passing tree**, shows the basic routes that most teams use. Teams might call these routes by different names, but all QBs and receivers need to know the different "branches" of the passing tree.

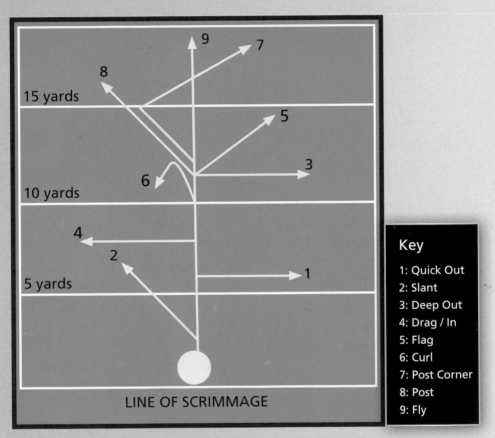

15 yards

10 yards

5 yards

LINE OF SCRIMMAGE

Key

1: Quick Out
2: Slant
3: Deep Out
4: Drag / In
5: Flag
6: Curl
7: Post Corner
8: Post
9: Fly

Tune In!

Watching football on TV can help build your QB skills. Even better, go to some games, from high school to the pros. Watching other quarterbacks in action will help you become the best QB you can be!

GLOSSARY

passing tree: a diagram that shows different routes, or patterns, that a receiver runs

Record Book

Who's the best of the best? Here are the top five performers in some key passing categories.

Passing Yards, Career
1. Brett Favre: 65,127 yards
2. Dan Marino: 61,361 yards
3. John Elway: 51,475 yards
4. Warren Moon: 49,325 yards
5. Fran Tarkenton: 47,003 yards

Passing Yards, Season
1. Dan Marino: 5,084 yards (1984)
2. Drew Brees: 5,069 yards (2008)
3. Kurt Warner: 4,830 yards (2001)
4. Tom Brady: 4,806 yards (2007)
5. Dan Fouts: 4,802 yards (1981)

▶ Drew Brees of the New Orleans Saints cracked the all-time top five with a team-record 5,069 yards in 2008.

Passing Yards, Game

1. Norm Van Brocklin, Rams: 554 yards (1951)
2. Warren Moon, Oilers: 527 yards (1990)
3. Boomer Esiason, Cardinals: 522 yards (1996)
4. Dan Marino, Dolphins: 521 yards (1998)
5. Phil Simms, Giants: 513 yards (1985)

▼ Brett Favre threw 22 touchdown passes in 2008. It was his only season with the New York Jets.

Touchdown Passes, Career

1. Brett Favre: 464
2. Dan Marino: 420
3. Fran Tarkenton: 342
4. Peyton Manning: 333
5. John Elway: 300

Touchdown Passes, Season

1. Tom Brady: 50 (2007)
2. Peyton Manning: 49 (2005)
3. Dan Marino: 48 (1984)
4. Dan Marino: 44 (1986)
5. Kurt Warner: 41 (1999)

Touchdown Passes, Game

These players each had seven TD passes in one game!

1. Sid Luckman, Bears (1943)
2. Adrian Burk, Eagles (1954)
3. George Blanda, Oilers (1961)
4. Y.A. Tittle, Giants (1962)
5. Joe Kapp, Vikings (1969)

*All records are through the 2008 season.

Glossary

audible: a new play that the QB calls at the line of scrimmage

bombs: long, high passes that often lead to touchdowns

bootleg: a run by the QB around the end of the line

defensive back: a defensive player who is usually assigned to cover a receiver

end-around: a running play in which a wide receiver takes a handoff from the quarterback

first-down marker: the pole on the sideline that shows where a team must reach to earn a first down

formations: the ways that football teams line up their players on the field

huddle: the gathering of a team's players before each play

interception: a pass that is caught by the defense

lateral: a pass that travels backward. A team is allowed one forward pass per play, but there is no limit on laterals.

line of scrimmage: the imaginary line that divides the offense and the defense before each play

NFL Draft: a yearly meeting in which NFL teams select from the top college players

overtime: an extra period that is played when a game is tied after 60 minutes

passing tree: a diagram that shows different routes, or patterns, that a receiver runs

pocket: the area that blockers form around the quarterback when he drops back to pass

Pro Bowl: the NFL's annual all-star game

quick release: for a QB, the ability to throw a pass before the defense reaches him

rookie: a player in his first season of pro football

route: the path a receiver takes as he goes out for a pass

scrambled: ran away from pass rushers

shotgun formation: a way that the offense lines up with the quarterback standing several feet behind the center

snap count: the words or numbers a QB calls out to start each play

sneak: a short run or plunge by the quarterback into the center of the line

two-minute drill: a series of plays run late in the half or game that help a team move the ball quickly

Find Out More

Books

Buckley, James, Jr. *Eyewitness Football*. New York: DK Publishing, 1999

Gigliotti, Jim. *Tom Brady*. Mankato, Minn.: Child's World, 2006

Leonetti, Mike. *In The Pocket: Johnny Unitas and Me*. San Francisco: Chronicle Books, 2008

Polzer, Tim. *Play Football!* New York: DK Publishing, 2003

Stewart, Mark. *The Ultimate 10: Football*. Pleasantville, N.Y.: Gareth Stevens, 2009.

Web Sites

www.nfl.com
> The official web site of the National Football League is packed with stats, video, news, and player bios. Football fans will find all they need about their favorite players and teams here.

www.nflrush.com
> It's the official kids' site of the NFL. Meet star players, see video of great plays, and get tips from the pros!

Publisher's note to educators and parents: Our editors have carefully reviewed these web sites to ensure that they are suitable for children. Many web sites change frequently, however, and we cannot guarantee that a site's future contents will continue to meet our high standards of quality and educational value. Be advised that children should be closely supervised whenever they access the Internet.

Index

About the Author

K.C. Kelley has written nearly two dozen books on sports for young readers. He has written about football, baseball, soccer, and NASCAR. He is a former editor with the NFL and *Sports Illustrated*.